Earth-Friendly Crafts in **5** Easy Steps

Earth-Friendly Papier-Mâché Crafts in 5 Easy Steps

Anna Llimós

Enslow Elementary
an imprint of
Enslow Publishers, Inc.
40 Industrial Road
Box 398
Berkeley Heights, NJ 07922
USA
http://www.enslow.com

Note to Kids and Parents: Getting earth-friendly materials is easy to do. Just look around your house for containers, wrappers, and other things you would throw out. Some of these recyclable materials may include plastic, paper, cardboard, cork, and cloth. The materials used in this book are suggestions. If you do not have an item, use something similar. Use any color material and paint that you wish. Use your imagination!

Safety Note: Be sure to ask for help from an adult, if needed, to complete these crafts.

Enslow Elementary, an imprint of Enslow Publishers, Inc.

Enslow Elementary® is a registered trademark of Enslow Publishers, Inc.

Translated from the Spanish edition by Stacey Juana Pontoriero.
Edited and produced by Enslow Publishers, Inc.

To Our Readers: We have done our best to make sure all Internet addresses in this book were active and appropriate when we went to press. However, the author and the publishers have no control over and assume no liability for the material available on those Internet sites or on other Web sites they may link to. Any comments or suggestions can be sent by e-mail to comments@enslow.com or to the address on the back cover.

Library of Congress Cataloging-in-Publication Data
Llimós Plomer, Anna.
  [Papel maché (2007). English]
  Earth-friendly papier-mâché crafts in 5 easy steps / Anna Llimós.
      pages cm — (Earth-friendly crafts in 5 easy steps)
  Translation of: Papel maché / Anna Llimós. — 1a ed. — Barcelona : Parramón Paidotribo, 2007.
  Translated from the Spanish edition by Stacey Juana Pontoriero.
  Includes bibliographical references and index.
  Summary: "Provides step-by-step instructions on how to create fourteen simple crafts using papier-mâché"—Provided by publisher.
  ISBN 978-0-7660-4192-9
  1. Papier-mâché—Juvenile literature. I. Title.
  TT871.L58313 2013
  745.54'2—dc23
                              2012013436

Future edition:
Paperback ISBN 978-1-4644-0315-6

Originally published in Spanish under the title *Papel maché*.
Copyright © 2007 Parramón Paidotribo-World Rights
Published by Parramón Paidotribo, S.L., Badalona, Spain

Production: Sagrafic, S.L.
Text: Anna Llimós
Illustrator: Nos & Soto

Printed in Spain
112012 Indice, S.L., Barcelona, Spain
10 9 8 7 6 5 4 3 2 1

Contents

Star

MATERIALS

papier-mâché
bowl of water
star-shaped plastic sand mold
white glue
paintbrush
paint–different colors
sponge

1 Dip pieces of papier-mâché in water and fill the mold. Brush some glue onto the side of the papier-mâché not touching the mold.

2 Press down on the papier-mâché so it takes the shape of the mold. Fold in the pieces that stick out. Let it dry.

3 Once dry, gently remove the star from the mold.

4 Paint it any way you wish. Let it dry.

5 Use a sponge dipped in paint to create more details. Let dry.

Use different sand molds to create fun critters!

5

Dancer

MATERIALS

papier-mâché
bowl of water
1 plastic funnel
white glue
paintbrush
air-drying clay
wire
paint—different colors
tissue paper

1 Tear the papier-mâché into pieces and dip them in water. As you add each piece to the funnel, brush some glue onto the paper. Be careful not to get glue on the funnel. Cover the funnel with the wet papier-mâché. Let dry.

2 Once dry and hard, gently remove the funnel. Roll out a long, thin piece of clay and cover a piece of wire in it. Place it on top of the funnel-shaped sculpture and bend it to make arms.

3 For the head, make a clay ball. Glue it on top of the arms and let dry. Paint the dress and let dry.

6

4 If you wish, you can add polka dots or any other decoration to the dress. Paint the face and arms. Let dry.

5 For the hair, roll tissue paper into long, thin pieces. Glue them to the head. Let dry.

What a lovely dancer!

7

Pencil Case

1 Cut out a cup from the egg carton. Place it at one end of the paper towel tube. Mix gluewash in the plastic bowl. Dip pieces of old newspaper in the gluewash. Wrap the wet strips of newspaper around the egg cup and tube. Let dry.

MATERIALS

egg carton
scissors
paper towel tube
gluewash (1/2 water, 1/2 glue)
small plastic bowl and spoon
(to mix gluewash)
old newspaper
air-drying clay
white glue
paint—different colors
paintbrush
strips of colored paper
ribbon
corrugated cardboard

2 Mold the pencil's lead from clay. Glue it to the egg cup and let dry.

3 Paint the pencil's lead and the wood. Let dry.

4 Dip strips of different colored paper in water. Brush some glue onto one side of each strip. Wrap the strips around the pencil. Add some ribbon. Let dry.

5 To make the stopper, roll a piece of corrugated cardboard until it is the same size as the hole.

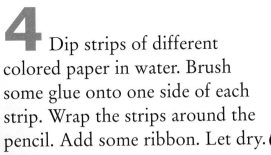

Keep your pencils inside!

Bracelets

1 Twist some old newspaper into a long, thin piece.

2 Wrap masking tape around it.

3 Attach the ends together to create the bracelet.

4 Cut tissue paper into little pieces.

5 Mix water and glue in the plastic bowl to make gluewash. Brush gluewash over the pieces of tissue paper to stick them around the bracelet. Let dry.

Make bracelets of all colors!

Fried Egg & Bread

1 Crumple some old newspaper into a ball. Attach it to one end of the toilet tissue tube with masking tape. Tear and twist some newspaper into three pieces. Tape them to the tube.

MATERIALS

old newspaper
2 toilet tissue tubes
masking tape
scissors
gluewash (1/2 water, 1/2 glue)
small plastic bowl and spoon
(to mix gluewash)
paint—different colors
paintbrush
sponge
papier-mâché
air-drying clay
white glue

2 For the slices, cut two rings from the other toilet tissue tube. Cover them with masking tape. Mix water and glue in the plastic bowl to make gluewash. Dip pieces of newspaper in the gluewash. Wrap them around the loaf and slices. Let dry.

3 Paint the bread crust. Use a sponge to paint the crumb so it looks toasted. Let dry.

4 For the fried egg, cut the shape of an egg white from papier-mâché. Roll a ball from clay to make the yolk. Glue the yolk to the center of the egg white and let dry.

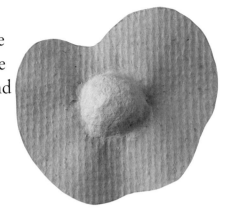

5 Paint the yolk and the egg white. Let dry.

They look
so real!

13

Butterfly

MATERIALS

wire
gluewash (1/2 water, 1/2 glue)
plastic bowl and spoon
(to mix gluewash)
paintbrush
tissue paper
air-drying clay
paint—different colors
white glue

1 To make wings, twist two pieces of wire into two figure eights. Attach them at the middle.

2 Mix water and glue in the plastic bowl to make gluewash. Brush tissue paper with gluewash. Cover the wings. Let dry.

3 Shape the body and two small balls from clay. To make the antennae, attach the balls to the body with wire.

4 Paint the body and antennae. Let dry.

5 Paint stripes or other decorations and the face. Let dry. Glue the body to the wings and let dry.

Let's fly!

Centipede

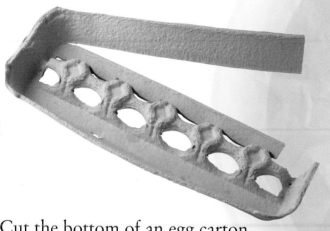

1 Cut the bottom of an egg carton as shown in the photograph.

2 Create the head out of clay. Stick the toothpicks in for the antennae.

3 Glue the head to the body and let dry.

16

4 Paint the body, head, and antennae as you wish. Let dry.

5 Decorate the body and draw the face.

So many legs!

Zebra

MATERIALS

old newspaper
2 toilet tissue tubes
masking tape
scissors
white glue
gluewash (1/2 water, 1/2 glue)
plastic bowl and spoon
(to mix gluewash)
paintbrush
paint–different colors
black felt

1 Stuff the toilet tissue tube with old newspaper. Have some newspaper hang out of one end to make the neck and head. Hold it all together with masking tape.

2 Cut the head and two ears from the other toilet tissue tube. Glue them to the neck and let dry.

3 For the legs and tail, twist some newspaper into two long pieces and one shorter piece. Tape them to the body. Mix water and glue in the plastic bowl to make gluewash. Dip pieces of newspaper in the gluewash. Cover the zebra in the wet pieces of newspaper, and let it dry.

4 Paint the body white or another color to make it more fun. Let it dry, then paint the eyes, nose, stripes, and hooves.

5 Create the mane out of black felt. Glue it onto the zebra and let dry.

Enjoy your new friend!

Salamander

1 Model the salamander from clay.

2 Dip pieces of old newspaper in water. As you add each piece to the clay salamander, brush some glue over the paper. Be careful not to get glue on the salamander. Let it dry and harden.

3 Gently remove the paper figure from the clay. Trim the edges.

4 Paint the salamander as you wish. Let dry.

5 Paint the eyes and mouth. Let dry.

What a cool salamander!

Swimmer

MATERIALS

old newspaper
masking tape
gluewash (1/2 water, 1/2 glue)
plastic bowl and spoon
(to mix gluewash)
air-drying clay
paint-different colors
paintbrush
raffia
scissors
white glue
blue card stock
white pencil

1 For the body, crumple some old newspaper into a ball. For the arms, twist some newspaper into a long, thin piece. Tape the arms to the body. Mix water and glue in the plastic bowl to make gluewash. Dip pieces of newspaper in the gluewash. Cover the body and arms with the wet newspaper. Let dry.

2 To make the inner tube, roll out a long, thick piece of clay. Wrap it around the body.

3 Mold the head and feet from clay.

22

4 Once everything is dry, paint it as you wish.

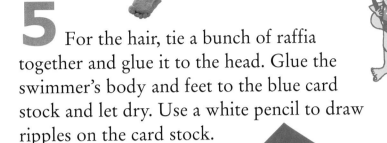

5 For the hair, tie a bunch of raffia together and glue it to the head. Glue the swimmer's body and feet to the blue card stock and let dry. Use a white pencil to draw ripples on the card stock.

Let's go swimming!

Stick Puppet

MATERIALS

air-drying clay
rope
1 wooden dowel
egg carton
scissors
gluewash (1/2 water, 1/2 glue)
plastic bowl and spoon
(to mix gluewash)
old newspaper
paint-different colors
paintbrush
tissue paper
white glue

1 Mold the head and hands out of clay. Attach the hands to the ends of a piece of rope. Tie the rope around the puppet's neck. Attach the head to the dowel.

2 Cut two cups from the egg carton. Run them through the dowel to make the body.

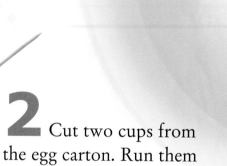

3 Mix water and glue in the plastic bowl to make gluewash. Dip some pieces of old newspaper in the gluewash. Wrap them around the egg cups. Let dry.

4 Paint the head and hands. Let dry.

5 Paint the body and face. Let dry. For the hair, glue a piece of crumpled tissue paper on top of the head.

Now you have a puppet to play with!

Bat

1 Make the body out of old newspaper and masking tape.

MATERIALS

old newspaper
masking tape
gluewash (1/2 water, 1/2 glue)
plastic bowl and spoon
(to mix gluewash)
black tissue paper
card stock—white and red
scissors
black permanent marker
white glue
papier-mâché
wire

2 Mix water and glue in the plastic bowl to make gluewash. Dip pieces of black tissue paper into the gluewash. Cover the body and let dry.

3 For the eyes, cut two small circles from white card stock. Use permanent marker to make the pupils. Cut a pair of fangs from red card stock. Glue the eyes and fangs onto the bat's face and let dry.

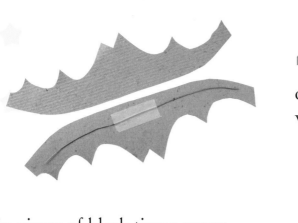

4 Draw two pairs of bat wings on a sheet of papier-mâché. Cut them out. Tape a piece of wire between them.

5 Dip pieces of black tissue paper into gluewash. Cover the wings. Once dry, glue them to the body. Let dry.

Move the wings!

Microphone

MATERIALS

old newspaper
plastic cup
masking tape
gluewash (1/2 water, 1/2 glue)
plastic bowl and spoon
(to mix gluewash)
small paper tube
white glue
paint-different colors
paintbrush
sponge
tissue paper

1 Crumple some old newspaper into a ball. Tape it to the plastic cup.

2 Mix water and glue in a plastic bowl to make gluewash. Dip some newspaper into the gluewash. Wrap it around the microphone. Let dry. Glue a small paper tube to the bottom of the plastic cup. Let dry.

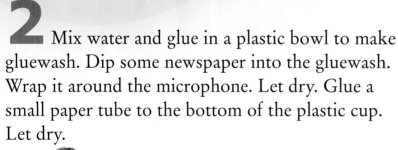

3 Paint the plastic cup and the paper tube. Let dry.

4 Paint the top of the microphone. Let dry. Use a sponge to add detail if you wish.

5 To make the microphone cable, twist a piece of tissue paper. Glue it to the inside of the paper tube. Let dry.

Sing!

Hat

MATERIALS

wrapping paper
plastic bowl
white glue
paintbrush
old magazine pages
scissors
gluewash (1/2 water, 1/2 glue)
plastic bowl and spoon
(to mix gluewash)
card stock
masking tape

1 Wet pieces of wrapping paper with water. Line the inside of the plastic bowl. Brush some glue onto the wrapping paper.

2 Fold in the pieces that stick out. Let dry. Gently remove the hardened paper from the bowl.

3 Find magazine pages with designs you like. Cut them into strips. Mix water and glue in a plastic bowl to make gluewash. Brush gluewash over the strips to stick them onto the hat. Let dry.

30

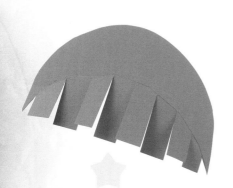

4 For the visor, cut a semicircle from card stock. Cut a fringe on one side. This will make it easier to attach it to the hat.

5 Glue the fringe of the visor to the inside of the hat. Use a few pieces of masking tape to keep the ends down.

You can wear it!

Read About

Books

The Bumper Book of Crafty Activities: 100+ Creative Ideas for Kids. Petaluma, Calif.: Search Press, 2012.

Hardy, Emma. *Green Crafts for Children.* New York: Ryland Peters & Small, 2008.

Henry, Sally. *Papier-Mâché.* London: Franklin Watts, 2011.

Internet Addresses

DLTK's Crafts for Kids: Paper Mache Crafts
<http://www.dltk-kids.com/type/papermache.htm>

Kids-Crafts-Creations: Paper Mache Crafts
<http://www.kids-crafts-creations.com/papermachecrafts.html>

Index

Easy to Hard